AWESOME
BUILDING GREAT RELATIONSHIPS

AWESOME: Building Great Relationships Study Guide

Published by Purpose Driven Communications.
23182 Arroyo Vista
Rancho Santa Margarita, CA 92688

Scripture quotations marked AMP are taken from the Amplified® Bible. Copyright © 1954, 1958, 1962, 1964, 1965, 1987 by The Lockman Foundation. Used by permission. (www.Lockman.org).

Scripture quotations marked ESV are taken from the ESV® Bible (The Holy Bible, English Standard Version®). Copyright © 2001 by Crossway, a publishing ministry of Good News Publishers. Used by permission. All rights reserved.

Scripture quotations marked GNT are taken from the Good New Translation in Today's English Version—Second Edition. Copyright 1992 by American Bible Society. Used by permission.

Scripture quotations marked LB are taken from The Living Bible. Copyright © 1971 by Tyndale House Publishers, Inc., Carol Stream, Illinois 60188. All rights reserved.

Scripture quotations marked NASB are taken from the New American Standard Bible®. Copyright © 1960, 1962, 1963, 1968, 1971, 1972, 1973, 1975, 1977, 1995 by The Lockman Foundation. Used by permission. (www.Lockman.org).

Scripture quotations marked NCV are taken from the New Century Version®. © 2005 by Thomas Nelson. Used by permission. All rights reserved.

All Scripture quotations, unless otherwise indicated, are taken from The Holy Bible, New International Version®, NIV®. Copyright © 1973, 1978, 1984, 2011 by Biblica, Inc.® Used by permission of Zondervan. All rights reserved worldwide. www.Zondervan.com. The "NIV" and "New International Version" are trademarks registered in the United States Patent and Trademark Office by Biblica, Inc.™ Except where otherwise noted, all references to NIV are from the 2011 version. Scriptures noted NIV* are from the 1984 version.

Scripture quotations marked NLT are taken from the Holy Bible, New Living Translation. © 1996, 2004, 2007, 2013, 2015 by Tyndale House Foundation. Used by permission of Tyndale House Publishers, Inc., Carol Stream, Illinois 60188. All rights reserved.

Scripture quotations noted ISV are from the The Holy Bible: International Standard Version. Release 2.0, Build 2015.02.09. Copyright © 1995-2014 by ISV Foundation. ALL RIGHTS RESERVED INTERNATIONALLY.

Scripture quotations marked [The Message] are taken from The Message. Copyright © by Eugene H. Peterson 1993, 1994, 1995, 1996, 2000, 2001, 2002. Used by permission of NavPress. All rights reserved. Represented by Tyndale House Publishers, Inc.

ISBN: 978-1-4228-0340-0

Printed and bound in the United States of America.

CONTENTS

Small Group Resources

AWESOME
BUILDING GREAT RELATIONSHIPS

UNDERSTANDING YOUR STUDY GUIDE

Here is a brief explanation of the features of this study guide.

CHECKING IN: You will open each meeting with an opportunity for everyone to check in with each other about how you are doing with the weekly assignments. Accountability is a key to success in this study!

KEY VERSE: Each week you will find a key verse or Scripture passage for your group to read together. If someone in the group has a different translation, ask them to read it aloud so the group can get a bigger picture of the meaning of the passage.

VIDEO LESSON: There is a video lesson for the group to watch together each week. Fill in the blanks in the lesson outlines as you watch the video, and be sure to refer back to these outlines during your discussion time.

DISCOVERY QUESTIONS: Each video segment is complemented by several questions for group discussion. Please don't feel pressured to discuss every single question. There is no reason to rush through the answers. Give everyone ample opportunity to share their thoughts. If you don't get through all of the discussion questions, that's okay.

PUTTING IT INTO PRACTICE: This is where the rubber meets the road. We don't want to be just hearers of the Word. We also need to be doers of the Word (James 1:22). These assignments are application exercises that will help you put into practice the truths you have discussed in the lesson.

PRAYER DIRECTION: At the end of each session you will find suggestions for your group prayer time. Praying together is one of the greatest privileges of small group life. Please don't take it for granted.

A Tip for the Host

The study guide material is meant to be your servant, not your master. The point is not to race through the sessions; the point is to take time to let God work in your lives. Nor is it necessary to "go around the circle" before you move on to the next question. Give people the freedom to speak, but don't insist on it. Your group will enjoy deeper, more open sharing and discussion if people don't feel pressured to speak up.

AWESOME
BUILDING GREAT RELATIONSHIPS

HOW TO USE THIS
VIDEO CURRICULUM

Follow these simple steps for a successful small group meeting:

- Open your group meeting by using the **Checking In** section of your study guide.

- Watch the video lesson together and follow along in the outlines in this study guide. Each video lesson is about 25 minutes long.

- Complete the rest of the discussion materials for each session. Be sure to review the **Putting It Into Practice** section and commit to fulfilling any action steps before your next session.

- Close your time together by following the **Prayer Direction** suggestions.

AWESOME
BUILDING GREAT RELATIONSHIPS

FIGHTING FOR AN
AWESOME MARRIAGE

CHECKING IN

Think about how marriage is portrayed in today's culture — in TV and movies and popular music, among celebrities, etc. How has that portrayal influenced how your view marriage?

KEY VERSE

"Marriage should be honored by everyone."

(HEBREWS 13:4a NCV)

▶ VIDEO OUTLINE

WHY MARRIAGE MATTERS

God created it ...

1) FOR THE _____ OF MEN AND WOMEN.

"In God's plan men and women need each other."
(1 CORINTHIANS 11:11b LB)

"It is not good for the man to be alone. I will make a companion who is right for him."
(GENESIS 2:18b)

"Jesus said, 'God's plan has been seen from the beginning of creation, when he made us male and female. This explains why a man leaves his father and mother and is joined to his wife, and the two are united as one body. Now since they are no longer two but one, no one should separate them for God has joined them together.'"
(MARK 10:6-9 NLT)

MARRIAGE IS _____ .

MARRIAGE IS _____ .

MARRIAGE IS _____ .

2) FOR THE _____ OF THE HUMAN RACE.

> *"So God created people in his own image; He patterned them after himself—creating both male and female with his image. Then God blessed them and commanded them, 'Be fruitful and multiply! Fill the earth!'"*
>
> (GENESIS 1:27-28a NLT)

> *"God, not you, made marriage. His Spirit inhabits even the smallest details of marriage. And what does he want from marriage? Godly children from your union. So guard the spirit of marriage within you."*
>
> (MALACHI 2:15 THE MESSAGE)

3) FOR THE _____ OF CHILDREN.

> *"Those who obey and respect the Lord have a secure fortress; their children will have a place of refuge and security."*
>
> (PROVERBS 14:26)

4) FOR THE _____ OF OUR CHARACTER.

"It's selfish and stupid to think only of yourself…"

(PROVERBS 18:1a CEV)

THE NUMBER ONE PURPOSE OF MARRIAGE IS TO
MAKE ME _____, NOT _____.

5) FOR THE _____ OF SOCIETY.

*"Righteousness lifts up a nation, but sin brings disgrace to
any society."*

(PROVERBS 14:34 GW)

6) FOR THE _____ OF OUR UNION
WITH CHRIST.

*"Husbands, love your wives as Christ loved the church and
gave himself up for her... He died so that he could give the
church to himself as a bride in all her beauty... In the same
way, husbands should love their wives as they love their own
bodies... No one ever hates his own body, but feeds and takes
care of it. And that is what Christ does for his church, his body.
The Scripture says, 'a man…is united with his wife, and the
two will become one body.' This is a profound mystery — but
I am talking about Christ and the church! So each husband
must love his wife as he loves himself, and each wife must
respect her husband."*

(EPHESIANS 5:25-33)

DISCOVERY QUESTIONS

1. One of the ways God uses marriage is for the perfection of our character. Using an example from your own life or the lives of a married couple you know, how have you seen God use marriage to shape character?

2. Mark 10:6-9 makes three radical statements about marriage: It's God's plan; it's between a man and a woman; and it's meant to be permanent. Which of these seems the most counter-cultural based on the way our society views marriage?

PUTTING IT INTO PRACTICE

Pastor Rick teaches that the number one purpose of marriage is to make us holy, not happy, and that our happiness comes as a byproduct of caring for our spouse first. As you think on your marriage or on the marriage you hope to one day have, what are some ways you can pursue holiness over happiness?

PRAYER DIRECTION

Discuss how your group wants to approach prayer during this six-week study. Encourage everyone to share his or her ideas. Ask if someone has a desire to be a prayer champion for the group, which could include summarizing and sending out prayer requests each week. Talk about other ways to support each other in prayer.

AWESOME
BUILDING GREAT RELATIONSHIPS

FIGHTING FOR AN
AWESOME FAMILY

CHECKING IN

Last week in session 1, Pastor
Rick taught how marriage
is meant to make us holy,
not happy.

For married couples: Were you
able to seek holiness in your
marriage this week? How did
caring for your spouse and
putting his or her needs over
your own affect your happiness?

For single men and women: Did
last week's session change the
way you think about and hope
for your future spouse?

KEY VERSE

*"Do not be afraid…
Remember the Lord, who
is great and awesome, and
fight for your brothers, your
sons, your daughters, your
wives, and your homes."*

(NEHEMIAH 4:14b ESV)

▶ VIDEO OUTLINE

4 TRAITS OF AWESOME FAMILIES

1) AWESOME FAMILIES ARE _____.

"I commend the enjoyment of life..."

(ECCLESIASTES 8:15a NIV)

"God, generously gives us everything for our enjoyment."

(1 TIMOTHY 6:17b GNT)

"People ought to enjoy every day of their lives, no matter how long they live."

(ECCLESIASTES 11:8a NCV)

"Enjoy life with your wife, whom you love..."

(ECCLESIASTES 9:9a NIV)

"Children are a gift from God."

(PSALM 127:3a LB)

"I recommend having fun... That way you will experience some happiness along with all the hard work God gives them."

(ECCLESIASTES 8:15 NLT)

2) AWESOME FAMILIES _____.

"Jesus grew in wisdom and stature, and in favor with God and with men."

(LUKE 2:52 NIV)

4 KINDS OF FAMILY GROWTH:

- Mental growth

- Physical growth

- Spiritual growth

- Social growth

WHAT DO WE LEARN FROM OUR FAMILIES?

1. WHAT TO DO WITH _____

2. HOW TO HANDLE _____

3. HOW TO HANDLE _____

   "Even if good people fall seven times, they will get back up."
   (PROVERBS 24:16 CEV)

4. WHAT VALUES _____

5. GOOD _____

HOW DO WE HELP EACH OTHER GROW?

- THROUGH _____

"Since I have washed your feet, you ought to wash each other's feet. I have given you an example to follow. Do as I have done to you."

(JOHN 13:14-15 NLT)

- THROUGH _____

"You must teach God's commandments to your children and talk about them when you are at home or out for a walk; at bedtime and the first thing in the morning."

(DEUTERONOMY 6:7 LB)

- NOT THROUGH _____

"Don't keep on scolding and nagging your children, making them angry and resentful. Instead bring them up with the loving training and teaching of the Lord."

(EPHESIANS 6:4b)

- NOT THROUGH _____

"Each person should judge his own actions and not compare himself with others. Then he can be proud for what he himself has done."

(GALATIANS 6:4 NCV)

"It rains on both those who do right and those who do wrong."

(MATTHEW 5:45b)

3) AWESOME FAMILIES _____.

"Two are better than one... If one of them falls down, the other can help him up. But if someone is alone and falls, it's just too bad, because there is no one to help him."

(ECCLESIASTES 4:9-10 GNT)

3 TYPES OF STORMS:

1. _____

2. _____

3. _____

4) AWESOME FAMILIES _____.

"Let us think about each other and help each other to show love and do good deeds."

(HEBREWS 10:24 NCV)

"He and all his family were devout and God-fearing; they gave generously to those in need and prayed to God regularly."

(ACTS 10:2 NIV)

"Do you remember Stephanas and his family? They were the first to become Christians in Greece, and they are spending their lives helping and serving Christians everywhere."

(1 CORINTHIANS 16:15 LB)

"Choose today whom you will serve… As for me and my family, we will serve the Lord."

(JOSHUA 24:15 NLT)

DISCOVERY QUESTIONS

1. Which of the "Four Traits of Awesome Families" is most challenging for you? Why?

2. Pastor Rick teaches that you spell love "T-I-M-E." Share an experience when giving your time to a family member turned out to be much more valuable than giving him or her a gift.

3. Has your family had to navigate one of the "Three Types of Storms"? How did you weather this storm together?

PUTTING IT INTO PRACTICE

Choose one of the "Four Traits of Awesome Families" that seems to be the biggest struggle for your family. Think of two or three practical steps that you can take to grow in this area, and come up with a plan to share these ideas with your family.

PRAYER DIRECTION

As you close in prayer, start by thanking God for your family and the ways he has helped you grow through your family members.

Then ask God to show you ways that your family needs to grow.

Finally, ask God for the courage to take the first steps in pursuing an awesome family.

AWESOME
BUILDING GREAT RELATIONSHIPS

FIGHTING FOR
AWESOME FRIENDSHIPS

CHECKING IN

Last week we talked about the first steps in becoming an awesome family. Share an experience you had this week with your family as you worked toward that goal.

KEY VERSE

"Do for others what you would like them to do for you! This summarizes all that's taught in the Law and Prophets."

(MATTHEW 7:12)

▶ VIDEO OUTLINE

WHY YOU NEED
AWESOME FRIENDS

- FOR _____

"I want us to help each other with the faith we have. Your faith will help me, and my faith will help you."

(ROMANS 1:12 NCV)

- FOR _____

"Carry each other's burdens, and in this way you will fulfill the law of Christ."

(GALATIANS 6:2 NIV)

- FOR _____

"Admit your faults to one another and pray for each other so that you may be healed."

(JAMES 5:16a LB)

- FOR _____

"God said, 'It is not good for man to be alone.'"

(GENESIS 2:18a LB)

- TO _____

"Two people are better than one, because they get more done by working together."

(ECCLESIASTES 4:9 NCV)

"Do for others what you would like them to do for you! This summarizes all that's taught in the Law and Prophets."

(MATTHEW 7:12)

6 GOLDEN RULES OF FRIENDSHIP

1) _____ THE TIME.

TO BE A FRIEND I HAVE TO _____!

2) _____ THEIR TRUST.

"Many people claim to be a friend, but it's rare to find someone who is truly trustworthy."

(PROVERBS 20:6)

HOW DO I EARN PEOPLE'S TRUST?

• BY _____

"A friend loves you all the time..."

(PROVERBS 17:17a NCV)

• BY _____

"A true friend is always loyal, and a brother is born to help in time of need."

(PROVERBS 17:17 LB)

"If you love someone, you'll be loyal to him no matter what the cost. You will always believe in him, always expect the best of him, and always stand your ground in defending him."

(1 CORINTHIANS 13:7 LB)

- BY _____

"...a true friend will keep a secret."

(PROVERBS 11:13b CEV)

"No one who gossips can be trusted ... but you can put your confidence in someone who is trustworthy."

(PROVERBS 11:13 GNT)

3) _____ WITH EMPATHY.

"We must bear the 'burden' of being considerate of the doubts and fears of others..."

(ROMANS 15:2a LB)

"A despairing man should have the devotion of his friends, even though he forsakes the fear of the Almighty."

(JOB 6:14)

4) _____ THEIR FLAWS.

"Accept each other just as Christ has accepted you; then God will be glorified."

(ROMANS 15:7 NLT)

"Overlooking a person's faults cultivates love; but nagging about them destroys friendships."

(PROVERBS 17:9)

5) _____ WINS, AND _____ LOSSES.

"Rejoice with those who rejoice; mourn with those who mourn."

(ROMANS 12:15 NIV)

6) _____ THEIR BEST.

YOUR BEST FRIEND IS THE PERSON WHO BRINGS OUT THE BEST IN YOU.

"A truly good friend will openly correct you. You can trust a friend who corrects you…"

(PROVERBS 27:5-6a CEV)

DISCOVERY QUESTIONS

1. One of the reasons we need awesome friends is for spiritual growth. Share an experience when a friend helped you grow spiritually.

2. Pastor Rick teaches that true friends are trustworthy. How have your closest friends earned your trust? Do you seek to earn their trust in the same ways?

3. Proverbs 27:5-6 says that a true friend will correct you. Do you have people in your life who will correct you if you're making a bad decision? Do you have a friend who trusts you enough to let you correct him or her?

PUTTING IT INTO PRACTICE

How can you be a better friend this week? Pick one of the "Golden Rules of Friendship" to practice this week with your closest friends as well as anyone else you know who might be in need of a friend.

PRAYER DIRECTION

As you begin your prayer time, ask God to bring to your mind anyone in your life who needs a friend this week. Then ask God to show you some practical ways that you can reach out to that person.

Finally, thank God for putting people in your life that you can depend on.

AWESOME
BUILDING GREAT RELATIONSHIPS

BECOMING BEST
FRIENDS WITH GOD

CHECKING IN

Last week we talked about how to have better friendships. Share with the group what steps you took toward being a better friend to those around you. Did you have a friend who was there for you in an unexpected way this week?

KEY VERSE

"I don't want your sacrifices — I want your love; I don't want your offerings — I want you to know me."

(HOSEA 6:6 LB)

▶ **VIDEO OUTLINE**

"...He is a God who is passionate about his relationship with you."

(EXODUS 34:14 NLT)

"I don't want your sacrifices — I want your love; I don't want your offerings — I want you to know me."

(HOSEA 6:6 LB)

"Starting from scratch, [God] made the entire human race and made the earth hospitable, with plenty of time and space for living so we could seek after God, and not just grope around in the dark but actually find him."

(ACTS 17:26-27 THE MESSAGE)

HOW TO BUILD A FRIENDSHIP WITH GOD

1) MAKE _____ MY #1 PRIORITY.

"Everything else is worthless compared with the priceless gain of knowing Christ Jesus. I've discarded everything else, counting it all as garbage, so that I may know Christ."

(PHILIPPIANS 3:8 NLT)

"You will find me when you seek me with all your heart."

(JEREMIAH 29:13)

I AM AS CLOSE TO GOD AS I CHOOSE TO BE.

2) _____ AND _____.

"Be still, and know that I am God."

(PSALM 46:10a NIV)

"Friendship with the Lord is reserved for those who reverence him. With them he shares the secrets of his covenant."

(PSALM 25:14)

"When you come before God, don't turn that into a theatrical production… Find a quiet, secluded place so you won't be tempted to role-play before God. Just be there as simply and honest as you can manage. The focus will shift from you to God, and you will begin to sense his grace."

(MATTHEW 6:5-6 THE MESSAGE)

3) DECIDE WHOSE _____ YOU WANT MOST.

"You should know that loving the world is the same as hating God. Anyone who wants to be a friend of the world becomes an enemy of God."

(JAMES 4:4 NCV)

"You are my friends if you obey me."

(JOHN 15:14 NLT)

"I have loved you as the Father has loved me... When you obey me, you remain in my love, just as I remain in my Father's love when I obey Him. I have told you this so that you'll be filled with my joy. Yes, your joy will overflow!"

(JOHN 15:9-11)

4) MAINTAIN A CONSTANT _____.

"Pray all the time."

(1 THESSALONIANS 5:17)

"My determined purpose is that I may know Him — that I may progressively become more deeply and intimately acquainted with Him, perceiving and recognizing and understanding the wonders of His Person more strongly and more clearly."

(PHILIPPIANS 3:10 AMP)

5) TRUST GOD IN _____.

> "Cast all your cares on the Lord and he will sustain you; he will never let the righteous fall."
>
> (PSALM 55:22)

IN TROUBLE?

> "I'll get you out of any trouble. I'll give you the best of care if you'll only get to know and trust me."
>
> (PSALM 91:14 THE MESSAGE)

DRIFTED AWAY FROM GOD?

> "In my early years, the friendship of God was felt in my home."
>
> (JOB 29:4)

> "If you return to me, I will restore you so you can continue to serve me. If you speak words that are worthy, you will be my spokesman. You are to influence them; do not let them influence you!"
>
> (JEREMIAH 15:19 NLT)

DISCOVERY QUESTIONS

1. Based on how you were raised, the concept of a friendship with God might be difficult to swallow. What preconceptions did you bring into the group today about the kind of relationship that's possible with God? Have you ever considered that God would actually want to be friends with you?

2. Pastor Rick teaches us that we have to make knowing God our number one priority. What's standing in the way of you putting God first in your life?

3. Which of the five ways to build a friendship with God is most challenging for you? What steps can you take this week to work toward that goal?

PUTTING IT INTO PRACTICE

As we wrap up this series, consider all the relationships in your life. Which ones are you the most thankful for? Have any relationships been neglected lately? Do any of your relationships need repairing or restoring?

Based on what you've learned through this series, come up with a plan to take the first steps toward focusing on any at-need relationships.

PRAYER DIRECTION

Start your prayer time in a spirit of thankfulness, thanking God for the people he has brought into your life and for the fact that he wants to have a friendship with you.

Ask God to reveal any relationships that need work, and ask him for the strength and courage to take those first steps toward restoration.

AWESOME
BUILDING GREAT RELATIONSHIPS

BONUS SESSION:
THE SEASONS OF MARRIAGE

NOTES

NOTES

NOTES

NOTES

NOTES

AWESOME
BUILDING GREAT RELATIONSHIPS

SMALL GROUP
RESOURCES

HELPS FOR HOSTS

TOP 10 IDEAS FOR NEW HOSTS

CONGRATULATIONS! As the host of your small group, you have responded to the call to help shepherd Jesus' flock. Few other tasks in the family of God surpass the contribution you will be making. As you prepare to facilitate your group, whether it is one session or the entire series, here are a few thoughts to keep in mind.

Remember you are not alone. God knows everything about you, and he knew you would be asked to facilitate your group. Even though you may not feel ready, this is common for all good hosts. God promises, *"I will never leave you; I will never abandon you"* (Hebrews 13:5 GNT). Whether you are facilitating for one evening, several weeks, or a lifetime, you will be blessed as you serve.

1. **DON'T TRY TO DO IT ALONE.** Pray right now for God to help you build a healthy team. If you can enlist a co-host to help you shepherd the group, you will find your experience much richer. This is your chance to involve as many people as you can in building a healthy group. All you have to do is ask people to help. You'll be surprised at the response.

2. **BE FRIENDLY AND BE YOURSELF.** God wants to use your unique gifts and temperament. Be sure to greet people at the door with a big smile . . . this can set the mood for the whole gathering. Remember, they are taking as big a step to show up at your house as you are to host a small group! Don't try to do things exactly like another host; do them in a way that fits you. Admit when you don't have an answer and apologize when you make a mistake. Your group will love you for it and you'll sleep better at night.

3. **PREPARE FOR YOUR MEETING AHEAD OF TIME.** Review the session and write down your responses to each question. Pay special attention to the Putting It Into Practice exercises that ask group members to do something other than engage in discussion. These exercises will help your group live what the Bible teaches, not just talk about it.

4. **PRAY FOR YOUR GROUP MEMBERS BY NAME.** Before you begin your session, take a few moments and pray for each member by name. You may want to review the Small Group Prayer and Praise Report at least once a week. Ask God to use your time together to touch the heart of each person in your group. Expect God to lead you to whomever he wants you to encourage or challenge in a special way. If you listen, God will surely lead.

5. **WHEN YOU ASK A QUESTION, BE PATIENT.** Someone will eventually respond. Sometimes people need a moment or two of silence to think about the question. If silence doesn't bother you, it won't bother anyone else. After someone responds, affirm the response with a simple "thanks" or "great answer." Then ask, "How about somebody else?" or "Would someone who hasn't shared like to add anything?" Be sensitive to new people or reluctant members who aren't ready to say, pray, or do anything. If you give them a safe setting, they will blossom over time. If someone in your group is a wallflower who sits silently through every session, consider talking to them privately and encouraging them to participate. Let them know how important they are to you—that they are loved and appreciated, and that the group would value their input. Remember, still water often runs deep.

6. **PROVIDE TRANSITIONS BETWEEN QUESTIONS.** Ask if anyone would like to read the paragraph or Bible passage. Don't call on anyone, but ask for a volunteer, and then be patient until someone begins. Be sure to thank the person who reads aloud.

7. **BREAK INTO SMALLER GROUPS OCCASIONALLY.** With a greater opportunity to talk in a small circle, people will connect more with the study, apply more quickly what they're learning, and ultimately get more out of their small group experience. A small circle also encourages a quiet person to

participate and tends to minimize the effects of a more vocal or dominant member.

8. **SMALL CIRCLES ARE ALSO HELPFUL DURING PRAYER TIME.** People who are unaccustomed to praying aloud will feel more comfortable trying it with just two or three others. Also, prayer requests won't take as much time, so circles will have more time to actually pray. When you gather back with the whole group, you can have one person from each circle briefly update everyone on the prayer requests from their subgroups. The other great aspect of subgrouping is that it fosters leadership development. As you ask people in the group to facilitate discussion or to lead a prayer circle, it gives them a small leadership step that can build their confidence.

9. **ROTATE FACILITATORS OCCASIONALLY.** You may be perfectly capable of hosting each time, but you will help others grow in their faith and gifts if you give them opportunities to host the group.

10. **ONE FINAL CHALLENGE (FOR NEW OR FIRST-TIME HOSTS).** Before your first opportunity to lead, look up each of the six passages listed below. Read each one as a devotional exercise to help prepare you with a shepherd's heart. Trust us on this one. If you do this, you will be more than ready for your first meeting.

"When Jesus saw the crowds, he had compassion on them, because they were harassed and helpless, like sheep without a shepherd. Then he said to his disciples, 'The harvest is plentiful but the workers are few. Ask the Lord of the harvest, therefore, to send out workers into his harvest field.'"

(MATTHEW 9:36–38 NIV)

'I am the good shepherd; I know my sheep and my sheep know me—just as the Father knows me and I know the Father—and I lay down my life for the sheep."

(JOHN 10:14–15 NIV)

"Be shepherds of God's flock that is under your care, serving as overseers—not because you must, but because you are willing, as God wants you to be; not greedy for money, but eager to serve; not lording it over those entrusted to you, but being examples to the flock. And when the Chief Shepherd appears, you will receive the crown of glory that will never fade away."

(1 PETER 5:2–4 NIV)

"If you have any encouragement from being united with Christ, if any comfort from his love, if any fellowship with the Spirit, if any tenderness and compassion, then make my joy complete by being like-minded, having the same love, being one in spirit and purpose. Do nothing out of selfish ambition or vain conceit, but in humility consider others better than yourselves. Each of you should look not only to your own interests, but also to the interests of others. Your attitude should be the same as that of Jesus Christ."

(PHILIPPIANS 2:1–5 NIV)

"Let us hold unswervingly to the hope we profess, for he who promised is faithful. And let us consider how we may spur one another on toward love and good deeds. Let us not give up meeting together, as some are in the habit of doing, but let us encourage one another—and all the more as you see the Day approaching."

(HEBREWS 10:23–25 NIV)

"...but we were gentle among you, like a mother caring for her little children. We loved you so much that we were delighted to share with you not only the gospel of God but our lives as well, because you had become so dear to us.... For you know that we dealt with each of you as a father deals with his own children, encouraging, comforting and urging you to live lives worthy of God, who calls you into his kingdom and glory."

(1 THESSALONIANS 2:7–8, 11–12 NIV)

FREQUENTLY ASKED QUESTIONS

How long will this group meet?

This study is four sessions long. We encourage your group to add a session for a celebration. In your final session, each group member may decide if he or she desires to continue on for another study. At that time you may also want to do some informal evaluation, discuss your group guidelines, and decide which study you want to do next. We recommend you visit our website at PastorRick.com for more video-based small group studies.

Who is the host?

The host is the person who coordinates and facilitates your group meetings. In addition to a host, we encourage you to select one or more group members to lead your group discussions. Several other responsibilities can be rotated, including refreshments, prayer requests, worship, or keeping up with those who miss a meeting. Shared ownership in the group helps everybody grow.

Where do we find new group members?

Recruiting new members can be a challenge for groups, especially new groups with just a few people, or existing groups that lose a few people along the way. We encourage you to use the Circles of Life diagram on page 54 of this study guide to brainstorm a list of people from your workplace, church, school, neighborhood, family, and so on. Then pray for the people on each member's list. Allow each member to invite several people from their list. Some groups fear that newcomers will interrupt the intimacy that members have built over time. However, groups that welcome newcomers generally gain strength with the infusion of new blood. Remember, the next person you add just might become a friend for eternity. Logistically, groups find different ways to add members. Some groups remain permanently open, while others choose to open periodically, such as at the beginning or end of a study. If your group becomes too large for easy, face-to-face conversations, you can subgroup, forming a second discussion group in another room.

How do we handle the childcare needs in our group?

Childcare needs must be handled very carefully. This is a sensitive issue. We suggest you seek creative solutions as a group. One common solution is to have the adults meet in the living room and share the cost of a babysitter (or two) who can be with the kids in another part of the house.

Another popular option is to have one home for the kids and a second home (close by) for the adults. If desired, the adults could rotate the responsibility of providing a lesson for the kids. This last option is great with school-age kids and can be a huge blessing to families.

CIRCLES OF LIFE

SMALL GROUP CONNECTIONS

Discover Who You Can Connect in Community

Use this chart to help carry out one of the values in the Group Guidelines, to "Welcome Newcomers."

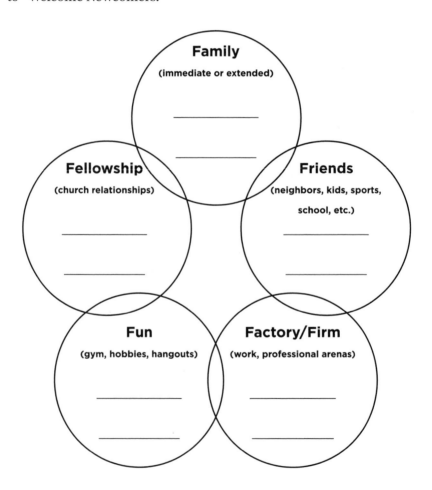

Follow this simple three-step process:

1. List one to two people in each circle.

2. Prayerfully select one person or couple from your list and tell your group about them.

3. Give them a call and invite them to your next meeting. Over 50 percent of those invited to a small group say, "Yes!"

GROUP GUIDELINES

It's a good idea for every group to put words to their shared values, expectations, and commitments. Such guidelines will help you avoid unspoken agendas and unmet expectations. We recommend you discuss your guidelines during Session 1 in order to lay the foundation for a healthy group experience. Feel free to modify anything that does not work for your group.

We agree to the following values:

CLEAR PURPOSE	To grow healthy spiritual lives by building a healthy small group community
GROUP ATTENDANCE	To give priority to the group meeting (call if I am absent or late)
SAFE ENVIRONMENT	To create a safe place where people can be heard and feel loved (no quick answers, snap judgments, or simple fixes)
BE CONFIDENTIAL	To keep anything that is shared strictly confidential and within the group
CONFLICT RESOLUTION	To avoid gossip and to immediately resolve any concerns by following the principles of Matthew 18:15–17

SPIRITUAL HEALTH

To give group members permission to speak into my life and help me live a healthy, balanced spiritual life that is pleasing to God

LIMIT OUR FREEDOM

To limit our freedom by not serving or consuming alcohol during small group meetings or events so as to avoid causing a weaker brother or sister to stumble (1 Corinthians 8:1–13; Romans 14:19–21)

WELCOME NEWCOMERS

To invite friends who might benefit from this study and warmly welcome newcomers

BUILDING RELATIONSHIPS

To get to know the other members of the group and pray for them regularly

OTHER

_____

_____

_____

We have also discussed and agree on the following items:

CHILDCARE   _____

STARTING TIME   _____

ENDING TIME   _____

If you haven't already done so, take a few minutes to fill out the Small Group Calendar on page 60.

SMALL GROUP PRAYER AND PRAISE REPORT

This is a place where you can write each other's requests for prayer. You can also make a note when God answers a prayer. Pray for each other's requests. If you're new to group prayer, it's okay to pray silently or to pray by using just one sentence:

"God, please help _____ to _____."

DATE	PERSON	PRAYER REQUEST	PRAISE REPORT

DATE	PERSON	PRAYER REQUEST	PRAISE REPORT

SMALL GROUP CALENDAR

Healthy groups share responsibilities and group ownership. It might take some time for this to develop. Shared ownership ensures that responsibility for the group doesn't fall to one person. Use the calendar to keep track of social events, mission projects, birthdays, or days off. Complete this calendar at your first or second meeting. Planning ahead will increase attendance and shared ownership.

DATE	LESSON	LOCATION	FACILITATOR	SNACK OR MEAL
	Session 1			
	Session 2			
	Session 3			

DATE	LESSON	LOCATION	FACILITATOR	SNACK OR MEAL
	Session 4			
	BONUS (optional)			
	Celebration			

ANSWER KEY

SESSION 1:
FIGHTING FOR AN AWESOME MARRIAGE

Why Marriage Matters: God created it...

1.) FOR THE **CONNECTION** OF MEN AND WOMEN.

   MARRIAGE IS **GOD'S PLAN**.

   MARRIAGE IS **BETWEEN A MAN AND A WOMAN**.

   MARRIAGE IS **PERMANENT**.

2.) FOR THE **MULTIPLICATION** OF THE HUMAN RACE.

3.) FOR THE **PROTECTION** OF CHILDREN.

4.) FOR THE **PERFECTION** OF OUR CHARACTER.

   THE NUMBER ONE PURPOSE OF MARRIAGE IS TO MAKE ME **HOLY**, NOT **HAPPY**.

5.) FOR THE **CONSTRUCTION** OF SOCIETY.

6.) FOR THE **REFLECTION** OF OUR UNION WITH CHRIST.

SESSION 2:
FIGHTING FOR AN AWESOME FAMILY

4 Traits of Awesome Families

1.) AWESOME FAMILIES ARE **PLAYFUL**.

2.) AWESOME FAMILIES **ENCOURAGE GROWTH**.

WHAT DO WE LEARN FROM OUR FAMILIES?

1. WHAT TO DO WITH **FEELINGS**

2. HOW TO HANDLE **CONFLICT**

3. HOW TO HANDLE **LOSS**

4. WHAT VALUES **MATTER MOST**

5. GOOD **HABITS**

HOW DO WE HELP EACH OTHER GROW?

- THROUGH **EXAMPLE**

- THROUGH **CONVERSATIONS**

- NOT THROUGH **CRITICIZING**

- NOT THROUGH **COMPARING**

3.) AWESOME FAMILIES **PROTECT EACH OTHER**.

3 TYPES OF STORMS:

1. **CHANGE**

2. **HARMFUL IDEAS**

3. **REJECTION**

4.) AWESOME FAMILIES **SERVE GOD AND OTHERS**.

SESSION 3:
FIGHTING FOR AWESOME FRIENDSHIPS

Why You Need Awesome Friends

- FOR **SPIRITUAL GROWTH**

- FOR **EMOTIONAL SUPPORT**

- FOR **BETTER HEALTH**

- FOR **SOCIAL ENJOYMENT**

- TO **REACH YOUR GOALS**

6 Golden Rules of Friendship

1.) **INVEST** THE TIME.

  TO BE A FRIEND I HAVE TO **SHOW UP**!

2.) **EARN** THEIR TRUST.

  HOW DO I EARN PEOPLE'S TRUST?

  - BY **BEING RELIABLE**

  - BY **BEING LOYAL**

  - BY **KEEPING CONFIDENCES**

3.) **LISTEN** WITH EMPATHY.

4.) **ACCEPT** THEIR FLAWS.

5.) **CELEBRATE** WINS, AND **SHARE** LOSSES.

6.) **BRING OUT** THEIR BEST.

SESSION 4:
BECOMING BEST FRIENDS WITH GOD

How to Build a Friendship with God

1.) MAKE **KNOWING GOD** MY #1 PRIORITY.

2.) **SLOW DOWN** AND **BE QUIET**.

3.) DECIDE WHOSE **FRIENDSHIP** YOU WANT MOST.

4.) MAINTAIN A CONSTANT **CONVERSATION**.

5.) TRUST GOD IN **YOUR PAIN**.

KEY VERSES

Session 1:

"Marriage should be honored by everyone."

(HEBREWS 13:4a NCV)

Session 2:

"Do not be afraid… Remember the Lord, who is great and awesome, and fight for your brothers, your sons, your daughters, your wives, and your homes."

(NEHEMIAH 4:14b ESV)

Session 3:

"Do for others what you would like them to do for you! This summarizes all that's taught in the Law and Prophets."

(MATTHEW 7:12)

Session 4:

"I don't want your sacrifices — I want your love; I don't want your offerings — I want you to know me."

(HOSEA 6:6 LB)

OTHER RECOMMENDED STUDIES

YOU MAKE ME CRAZY
6-Week Study

AVAILABLE AT PASTORRICK.COM/STORE

OTHER RECOMMENDED STUDIES

THE HABITS OF HAPPINESS
6-Week Study

AVAILABLE AT PASTORRICK.COM/STORE

OTHER RECOMMENDED STUDIES

THE KEYS TO A BLESSED LIFE
6-Week Study

AVAILABLE AT PASTORRICK.COM/STORE

OTHER RECOMMENDED STUDIES

FINANCIAL FITNESS
5-Week Study

AVAILABLE AT PASTORRICK.COM/STORE